Dear Parents,

Children are naturally curious about the world around them, and curiosity is a powerful motivation for reading. Studies show that informational reading is critical to success in school. National Geographic Kids Readers allow you to feed your children's interests and create readers who not only can read, but also want to read!

To sustain children's excitement about reading, we have created a special program called **NATIONAL GEOGRAPHIC KIDS SUPER READERS.** As kids read each National Geographic Kids Reader, they cross off its picture on a free National Geographic Kids Super Readers poster that parents can download from kids.nationalgeographic.com/superreaders.

Throughout the process, kids and parents go to the website and download specially designated prizes that reward their effort. Kids can have even more reading fun online, with lively book-related activities, quizzes and games, fascinating excerpts, and sneak previews of upcoming books.

The National Geographic Kids Super Readers program appeals to kids' love of accomplishment while providing them with incentives to keep reading. When the reading experience is fun, children learn more and achieve more. What could be better than that?

Sincerely,

Mariam Jean Dreher

Mariam Jean Dreher
Professor of Reading Education
University of Maryland, College Park

NATIONAL GEOGRAPHIC KiDS

$0.50

Halloween

Laura Marsh

Halloween

Laura Marsh

NATIONAL GEOGRAPHIC

Washington, D.C.

For Paige and Wyatt
—L. F. M.

Design by YAY! Design

Photo Credits
Cover, Picture Partners/Photo Researchers, Inc.; 1, Blend Images/SuperStock; 2, Klaus Kaulitzki/Shutterstock; 4, Ariel Skelley/Blend Images/Corbis; 6 (left), Comstock; 6 (top right), quavondo/Vetta/Getty Images; 6 (bottom right), Tim Kitchen/Digital Vision/Getty Images; page 6-7 (background), Abdus Shahed Chowdhury/NGMS; 7 (top left), Tony Campbell/Shutterstock; 7 (top right), Tahbar Junus/National Geographic My Shot; 7 (bottom), Ocean/Corbis; 8, Radius/SuperStock; 9, Lori Sparkia/Shutterstock; 10, Mark Thiessen, NGP; 11 (left), Mark Thiessen, NGP; 11 (top right), Bananastock/PictureQuest; 11 (bottom right), Photodisc Green/Getty Images; 12, Josh McCulloch/All Canada Photos/Corbis; 13 (top), Simon Krzic/Shutterstock; 13 (bottom left), Roger Phillips/Getty Images; 13 (bottom right), Corey Hochachka/Robertstock.com; 14, Blend Images/SuperStock; 15, Stockbyte/Getty Images; 16 (top), Robert Neumann/Shutterstock; 16 (bottom), Sergieiev/Shutterstock; 17 (top left), Courtesy DecoArt using Americana Acrylics; 17 (top right), Courtesy DecoArt using Americana Acrylics; 17 (bottom left), Courtesy DecoArt using Americana Acrylics; 17 (bottom right), Courtesy DecoArt using Americana Acrylics; 18 (top left), Brandon Blinkenberg/Shutterstock; 18 (top right), Michael C. Gray/Shutterstock; 18 (bottom), Bananastock/PictureQuest; 19 (top), AP Images/Seth Wenig; 19 (bottom right), Megapress/Alamy; 19 (bottom left), Denise Taylor/Flickr/Getty Images; 20, Mark Thiessen, NGP; 22 (top), Russell K. Scheid/Flickr/Getty Images; 22 (center), Barbara Ries; 22 (bottom), Brian Harkin; 23 (top left), Lisa Thornberg/iStockphoto; 23 (bottom left), Rob Kinmonth; 23 (right), Rebecca Richardson/Getty Images; 24, AFP/Getty Images; 26, I Love Images/Corbis; 29 (top), AP Images/Gregory Bull; 29 (bottom), Charles O. Cecil/Alamy; 30 (left), Hugo Chang/iStockphoto; 30 (right), Rick Seeney/Shutterstock; 31 (top left), Edward Westmacott/Shutterstock; 31 (top right), Nico Smit/iStockphoto; 31 (bottom left), Fong Kam Yee/Shutterstock; 31 (bottom right), Robert Neumann/Shutterstock; page 32 (top left), Ronald Sumners/Shutterstock; 32 (top right), AFP/Getty Images; 32 (bottom left), Blend Images/SuperStock; 32 (bottom right), Josh McCulloch/All Canada Photos/Corbis

**National Geographic supports K-12 educators with
ELA COMMON CORE RESOURCES.
Visit www.natgeoed.org/commoncore**

Printed in the United States of America
18/WOR/5

Table of Contents

Halloween Fun!

Costumes, candy, trick-or-treating,
parties, games, and lots of eating.

Halloween just can't be beat—
it's a holiday that's one big treat!

Ghost and goblins,
pumpkins, too,
black cats, bats,
and witches' brew.

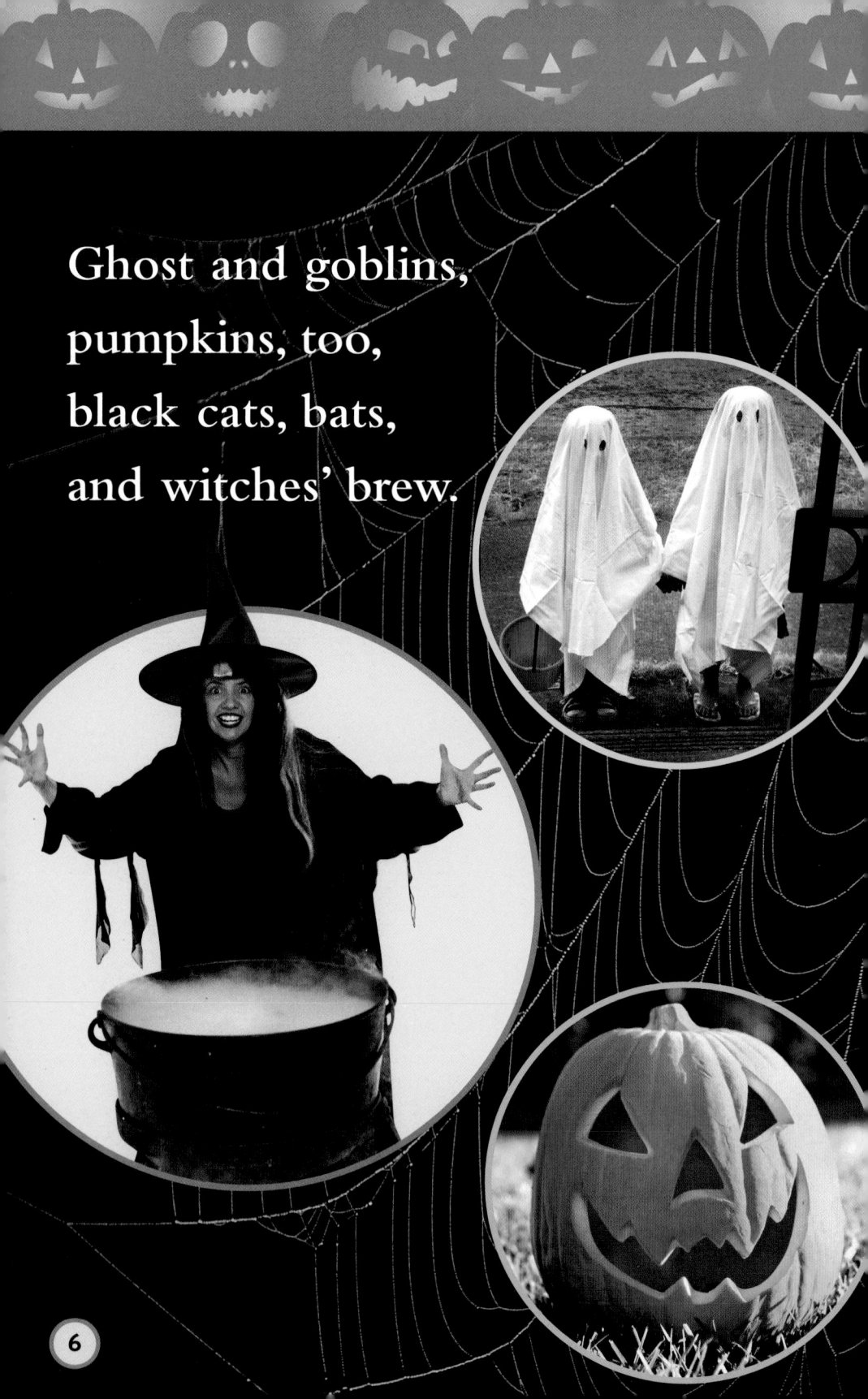

In October,
have you seen
all these things
on Halloween?

Trick-or-Treat

What's the best part about Halloween? Most kids would say trick-or-treating!

Going door-to-door for candy is lots of fun.

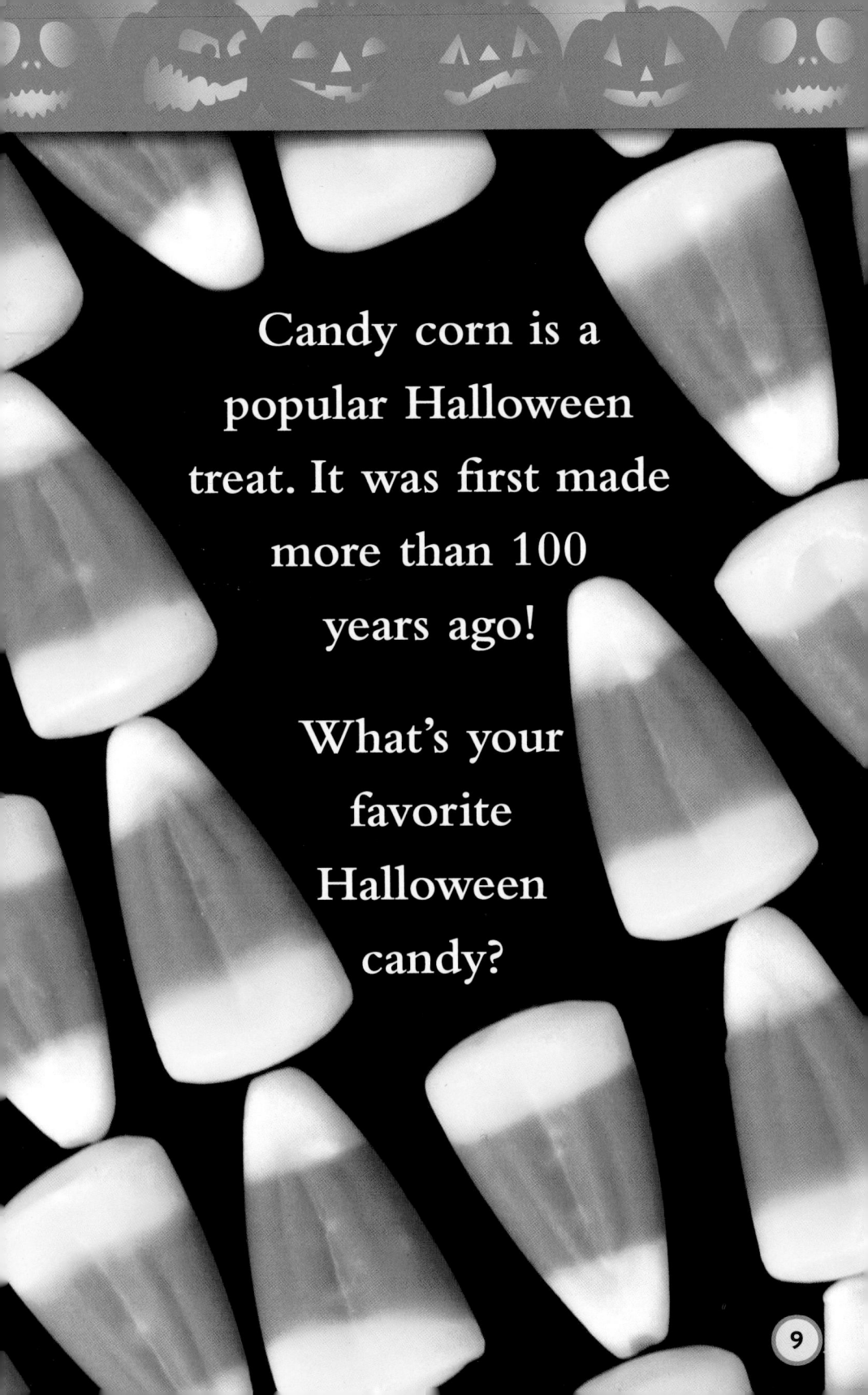

Candy corn is a popular Halloween treat. It was first made more than 100 years ago!

What's your favorite Halloween candy?

Costumes

What will you be for Halloween?
Will you be silly or scary,
something real or make-believe?

You can be almost anything.
How about . . .

a shark

a circus clown

a bat

a ghost

Pumpkin Picking

Do you know where pumpkins come from? A pumpkin patch!

TRICKY TERM

PATCH: A small piece of land where fruits and vegetables grow

seeds

A pumpkin grows from a seed. First a vine grows from the seed. Next the vine grows fruit— pumpkin fruit, that is!

vine

fruit

Pumpkins can be **BIG** or SMALL, **round** and **WIDE**, or **TALL** and skinny.

Jack-o'-lanterns

You can make a jack-o'-lantern! Draw a funny face on a pumpkin. Ask an adult to carve it for you. Then place a light inside.

We carve pumpkins in America. But jack-o'-lanterns started in Ireland. People there carved turnips, beets, or potatoes.

Painting Pumpkins

You can paint a pumpkin for Halloween!

Pumpkin faces can be silly or serious. They can be scary or friendly.

Q What does a skeleton order at a restaurant?

A Spareribs!

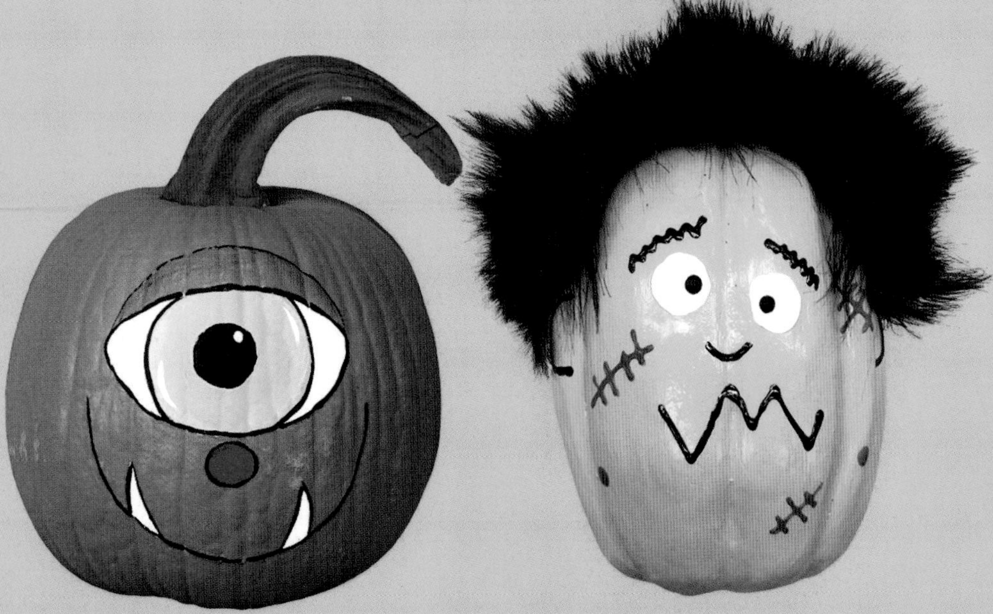

You can paint monsters, a pirate, or even a puppy.

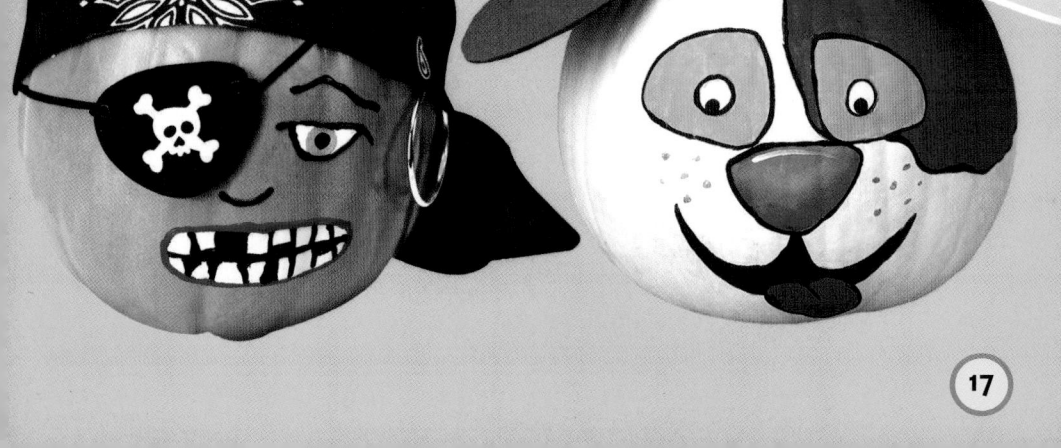

6 Halloween Fun Facts

1

Each pumpkin has about 500 seeds.

2

3

Most parents say they eat candy from their kids' Halloween bags.

The most popular costumes are witches, princesses, and superheroes.

4

The world's largest pumpkin had to be lifted by a tractor!

5

Half of Americans decorate their homes for Halloween.

6

Pumpkins can be orange, red, green, yellow, blue, tan, or white.

A Spooky Home

Give trick-or-treaters a creepy welcome on Halloween night. Here are some ideas:

Cover bushes with fake spiderwebs.

Play spooky music.

R.I.

Decorate your doorway with black paper bats.

Hang a skeleton or ghost in a window.

Pet Parade

Why should people have all the fun? Pets can dress up, too!

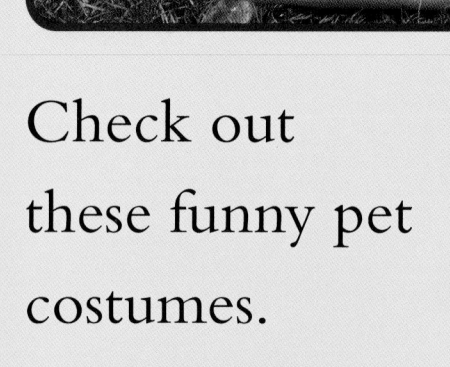

Check out these funny pet costumes.

Halloween candy is not safe for pets. Make sure pets only eat treats made just for them.

First Halloweens

Halloween traditions started in ancient times. People dressed in costumes. They lit fires. They believed this would scare away ghosts.

October 31 was later called All Hallows' Eve. That's how we got the name Halloween.

TRICKY TERM

TRADITION: A way of doing something that is passed from older family members to children

ANCIENT: From a long time ago, very old

25

Halloween Today

Halloween is a mix of these traditions and many others. They come from Europe, North America, and South America. But most of all, Halloween is a day for fun!

Q How do you fix a broken jack-o'-lantern?

A With a pumpkin patch!

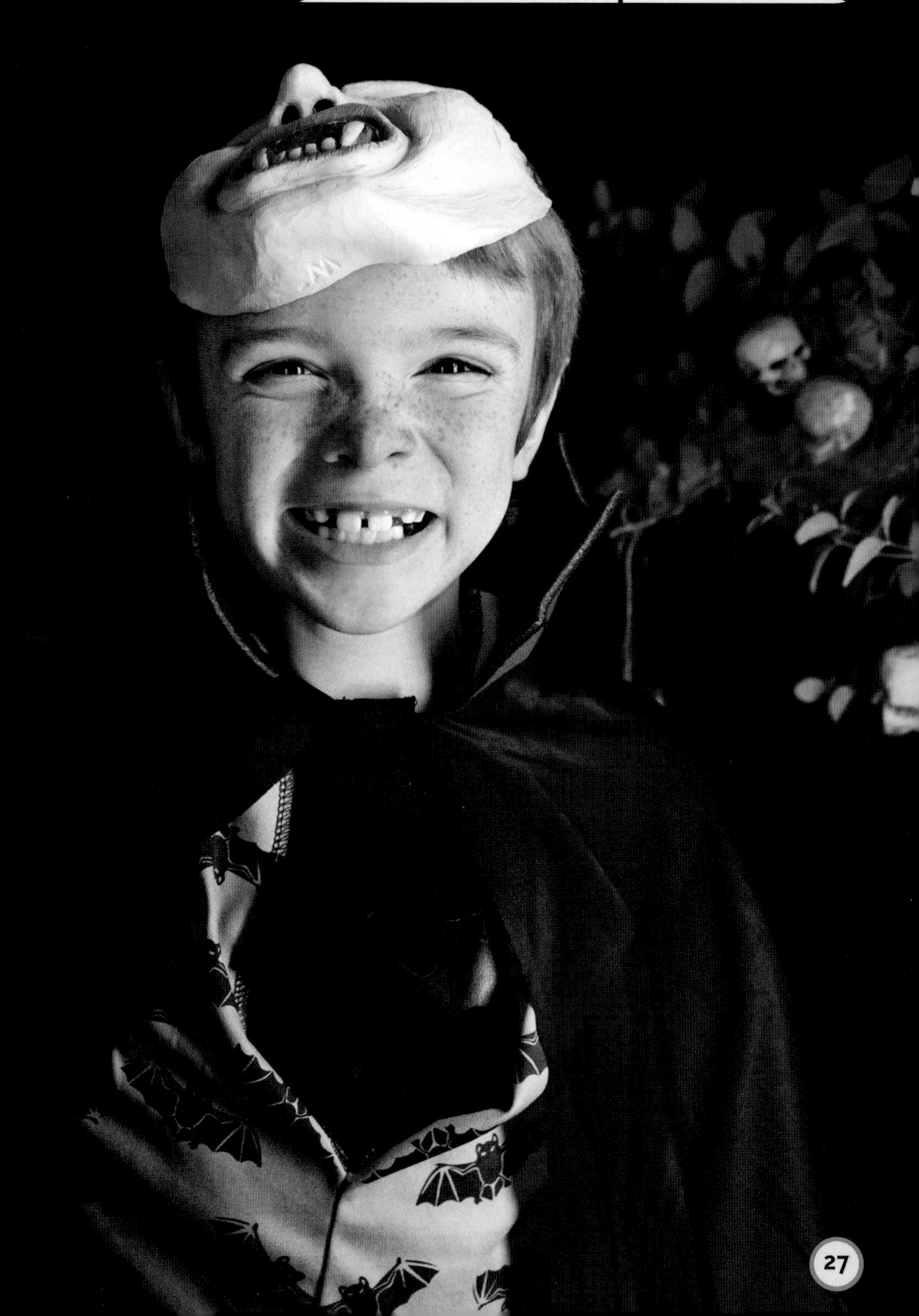

Day of the Dead

Instead of Halloween, some people around the world celebrate the Day of the Dead. It's similar to Halloween. But it's different, too.

Families honor loved ones who have died. They make special food. They decorate graves. Sometimes children dress in skeleton costumes. They also eat skull-shaped candy.

TRICKY TERM

HONOR: To show respect for someone or something

Decorating a grave with flowers in Mexico

The Day of the Dead is called Día de los Muertos (DEE-ah DAY lohs MWER-tos) in Spanish.

candy sugar

What in the World?

These pictures show close-up views of Halloween objects. Use the hints to figure out what's in the pictures. Answers are on page 31.

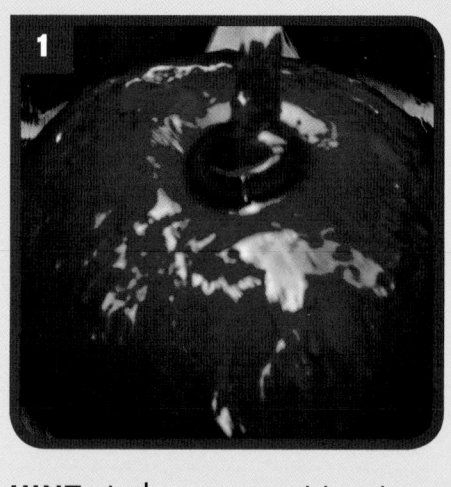

HINT: A chewy, sweet treat on a stick

HINT: A pumpkin grows from one of these.

WORD BANK

jack-o'-lantern   seeds   spider   pumpkin
candy apple   bat

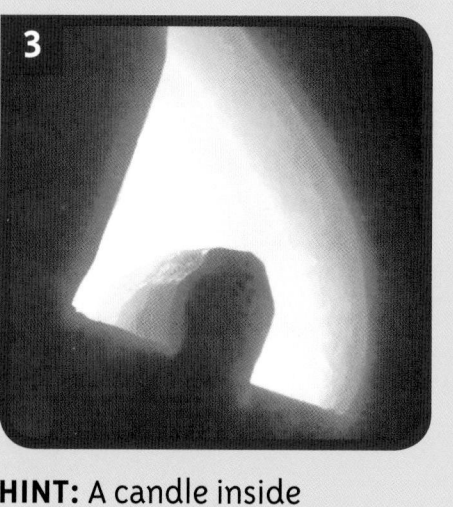

3

HINT: A candle inside makes it glow.

4

HINT: It sleeps upside down.

5

HINT: It spins a web.

6

HINT: Most are orange, but they can be other colors, too.

Answers: 1. candy apple, 2. seeds, 3. jack-o'-lantern, 4. bat, 5. spider, 6. pumpkin

ANCIENT: From a long time ago, very old

HONOR: To show respect for someone or something

TRADITION: A way of doing something that is passed from older family members to children

PATCH: A small piece of land where fruits and vegetables grow